TROPICAL Rain Forest ADVENTURE

Welcome to the Rain Forest

by Julia Osborne

Where can you find the greatest variety of living things? You can find it in a tropical rain forest.

If you want to visit one, travel toward the Equator. It is mostly warm there. And at least 250 cm (100 inches) of rain fall every year.

The largest rain forest in the world grows near the Amazon River in South America. Millions of plants and animals live there. Scientists have discovered many of them. Even more are yet to be discovered.

Equator

The Amazon rain forest is the largest rain forest on Earth.

The Emergent Layer

Rain forest plants grow in four different layers. The highest layer is called the **emergent layer.** Tall trees rise above the rest of the forest.

Trees in the emergent layer get the most sunlight. The weather is hot and windy. Heavy rain and lightning are common.

The harpy eagle lives in the tallest trees. It catches large monkeys. Then it eats them!

The blue morpho butterfly often flies above the treetops.

The white-throated toucan has a very large bill. Its bill helps it eat fruit, insects, and lizards.

The Canopy

Below the emergent layer is the **canopy.** It is like the roof of the forest. Tree branches and leaves grow close together. The leaves use energy from sunlight to make food for the trees.

Many animals eat the trees' leaves. They also eat their fruits and seeds. Other animals eat the animals that eat plants. Many animals that live in the canopy never go to the ground.

The canopy is the busiest layer of the rain forest. What a racket! Parrots squawk. Toucans croak. Frogs peep. Bees buzz. The wings of beetles click and whirr.

The most common animals in the canopy are insects. The most common insects are beetles. A scientist found more than 900 different kinds of beetles on just one tree!

A red howler monkey opens its mouth wide. ROAR! The monkey sounds scary. But it eats mostly leaves and fruits.

This three-toed sloth moves very s-l-o-w-l-y. It has green algae in its hair. That helps the sloth blend in with the leaves.

Some beetles of the Amazon

Tortoise beetle   Rhinoceros beetle

Jewel beetle   Rhinastus weevil

5

The Understory

The **understory** is below the canopy. Small trees and shrubs grow in this layer.

The canopy blocks the sunlight. This makes the understory dim. Many plants have huge leaves. These leaves capture the small amount of light that comes through the canopy.

Watch out! There are dangerous animals here. Scorpions sting. Ants bite. Spiders spin sticky webs. Powerful jaguars jump on other animals.

An emerald boa constrictor is ready to catch a bird or a mouse.

The pygmy marmoset licks the sweet sap that comes out of trees.

Poison dart frogs have poison in their skin. The poison has been used to make poisoned arrows.

Rain Forest Food Chain

The different layers of the rain forest are linked together by **food chains.** A food chain shows how energy passes from one kind of living thing to another.

The Brazil-nut tree gets energy from sunlight. It uses energy to make Brazil nuts.

The agouti gets energy by eating Brazil nuts. It is the only animal that can chew open the hard part around the Brazil nuts.

The jaguar gets energy by eating smaller animals, such as agoutis.

The green anaconda is the heaviest snake in the world. It wraps its body around its prey. Then it squeezes until its prey cannot breathe.

The Forest Floor

Did you bring a flashlight? It can be very dark on the forest floor. Only a few shrubs, ferns, and grasses grow here. Leaves, fruits, and seeds drop from the canopy. Ants and termites crawl on the ground. Fungi and bacteria break down dead things.

Surprise! Rain forest soil is not very rich. Dead things decay quickly. Nutrients from decaying plants and animals are taken up by tree roots. Few nutrients are left in the thin soil.

The Brazilian tapir has a wiggly snout. It sniffs out food. Only young tapirs have stripes.

The bird-eating tarantula can be nearly as big as a dinner plate.

A casque-headed frog opens its huge mouth. Then it snaps at an enemy.

Check In What are the four layers of the rain forest? List an animal from each layer.

GENRE **Third-Person Narrative**

Read to find out how a field biologist takes pictures of animals at night.

Tim Laman
NIGHT IN THE RAIN FOREST

by Julia Osborne

It's evening on the island of Borneo. Tim Laman is heading into the rain forest.

Why go at night? That's when many animals wake up! Tim tells us why. "At night the rain forest is as rich in life as it is by day, but with an almost completely different cast of characters."

Bats, owls, and moths hide during the day. They start moving when the sun sets. These animals are **nocturnal.** They are active at night.

Tim photographed the animals in this story. It took him many months. Often he stayed awake all night. "I went totally nocturnal for weeks, staying out in the forest until the first hint of dawn," he says.

Equator

Borneo is a huge island in the Pacific Ocean near Southeast Asia.

TIM LAMAN is a photographer and field biologist. He studies the wildlife in places such as rain forests and coral reefs. His photographs have won him many awards. He hopes his photos will inspire people to save rain forests and other natural places.

Perched in a tall tree, Tim gets ready to take pictures at night.

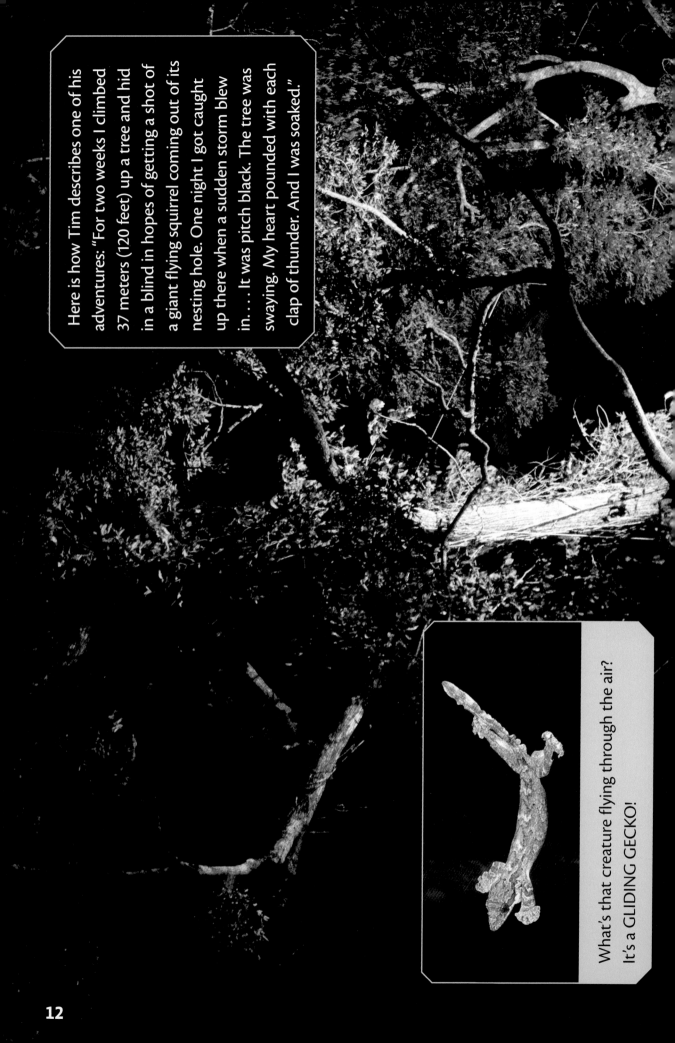

Here is how Tim describes one of his adventures: "For two weeks I climbed 37 meters (120 feet) up a tree and hid in a blind in hopes of getting a shot of a giant flying squirrel coming out of its nesting hole. One night I got caught up there when a sudden storm blew in. . . . It was pitch black. The tree was swaying. My heart pounded with each clap of thunder. And I was soaked."

What's that creature flying through the air? It's a GLIDING GECKO!

Gliding Through the Forest

Borneo has more kinds of gliding animals than any other place on Earth. These animals don't have wings. They can't really fly. They glide from tree to tree.

Gliders usually live in treetops. No one had ever taken pictures of them in action. Some people thought it would be too hard. Tim was up for the challenge.

Sometimes Tim climbed up to the **canopy.** This layer of leaves is high above the forest floor. Tim brought his cameras. He built a hiding place called a blind. Then he waited and waited. He waited for a glider to come close. Then he snapped its picture.

Tim took this picture of a Wallace's flying frog as one glided to the ground. "It was exciting to see something that very few people have seen before. To capture it on film was a real high point."

Light up the Night

What is the rain forest like at night? Tim says, "Whether I am strolling along a forest track or making a nighttime climb of a dipterocarp tree, the night has many surprises. . . . On a moonless, overcast night, I turn off my headlamp and stand among the towering trees of Borneo's lowland forest. At first it seems as black as the deepest cave. But as my eyes adjust, I see that the forest has some light of its own."

Flash! A plant hopper is captured in a nighttime photo. The long "tail" of this insect is really poop! The plant hopper feeds on plant juices. Then it releases long waxy strands of waste.

To take pictures at night, Tim needs the right equipment. He uses flashlights, headlamps, and flashes on his cameras.

Tim continues, "A bright point of light nearby turns out to be a strange beetle larva called a starworm crawling among the leaves. Why does the starworm produce its steady glow? Could it be seeking a mate? Luring prey? For now it remains one of the many mysteries of the rain forest at night."

Tim uses a bright headlamp to see a lizard.

Super Senses

How do animals survive in the dark? They use their senses. They use sight, hearing, touch, and smell. "I wish my senses were a match for these nocturnal creatures," says Tim.

"One evening as I entered the forest, I smelled a heady perfume coming from a flower opening to attract small moths. Like many night-blooming plants, this orchid has pale flowers that are easy to spot in low light."

This is a tarsier. It lives on a large island near Borneo. Tarsiers have huge eyes, sharp ears, and a delicate sense of touch. They use these senses to find food. This tarsier is eating a cockroach. Yum!

Night is ending. The nocturnal animals look for safe resting places. Some hide in dark tree holes. Others crawl into cracks in bark. They wait for darkness to return.

Tim hurries home. It's time for him to get some sleep. He hears birds greet the new day. The daytime animals are waking up!

Check In How does Tim Laman take pictures of animals at night? What equipment does he use?

Saving the Rain Forests

by Julia Osborne

Why would anyone destroy a rain forest?

Some people cut down trees to make room for crops or cattle. Others sell the wood or make paper. Still others want to build roads and cities.

Earth's rain forests are in danger. More than half of them have been cut down or burned. Scientists are worried. If this continues, the rain forests could be gone in 100 years!

We need to save our rain forests. Animals need them. People need them. They are important to the environment.

Millions of plants and animals live in rain forests. When forests are cut down, the animals have no place to live. They might go **extinct.** This means that they would no longer live on Earth.

The land is harmed when trees are cut down. There are no roots to hold the soil in place. Wind and water carry the soil away. Floods destroy farms and villages.

Products We Need

Do you like bananas and chocolate? These foods come from rain forest plants.

People who live in rain forests depend on them for food, clothing, and shelter. People around the world get food and important products from rain forests, too.

Rain forest plants are used to make medicines. These medicines help people fight diseases.

Rain Forest Products

Tropical fruits such as bananas, guavas, mangoes, papayas, and passion fruit

Woods such as balsa, mahogany, and teak

Nuts such as Brazil nuts, cashews, kola nuts, and macadamia nuts

Rubber and fibers such as bamboo, ramie, and rattan

Flavorings such as cinnamon, coffee, chocolate, ginger, nutmeg, and vanilla

Medicines used to treat diseases such as arthritis, cancer, diabetes, heart disease, and malaria

This man's basket is full of Brazil nut capsules. Collecting them did not harm the forest.

RAINFOREST ALLIANCE CERTIFIED ™

This seal means that a product has been harvested sustainably.

Many products can be safely harvested from rain forests. **Sustainable harvesting** is safe for wildlife and people.

Brazil nuts can be harvested sustainably. People sell the nuts they collect from the forest floor. This saves trees. It also helps people make money.

Rain Forest Parks

Rain forests are AMAZING. Some countries set aside parts of rain forests as parks. Tourists can see the wildlife without harming the trees. Some people pay to stay in a rain forest. Their money helps the local people. It is also used to protect the forest.

Working Together

People should work together to save the world's rain forests. This will protect plants and animals from going extinct. It will help people get the products they need.

If we save our rain forests now, people will be able to enjoy them for centuries to come.

What you can do

You can help save the rain forests. It doesn't matter where you live.

- Use less paper. Recycle paper.

- Buy rain forest products that have been harvested sustainably.

- Do not buy pets from rain forests.

- Share what you know about rain forests. Encourage people to help save the rain forests.

Check In How are rain forests important to people around the world?

Discuss

1. How did the information in "Welcome to the Rain Forest" help you understand the other two pieces in the book?

2. Compare the canopy layer of a rain forest with the forest floor. How are they alike and different?

3. Think about the rain forest at night. How are animals able to find food in the dark? Give some examples.

4. Explain what will happen to the rain forest animals if the trees are cut down.

5. What do you still wonder about tropical rain forests? What would be some good ways to find out more?

3-D THRILLERS!

Jungle

PAUL HARRISON

ARCTURUS

W hen people say jungle, they usually mean tropical rainforest. Rainforests are found around the equator — the imaginary line that circles the middle of the earth. There are rainforests in Africa, Central and Southern America, Asia and Australia.

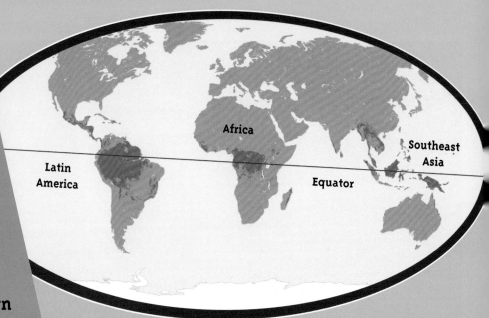

Latin
America

Africa

Southeast
Asia

Equator

◀ SAME BUT DIFFERENT

There are different types of tropical rainforest. The majority of the rainforest is called lowland forest, where it is warm all year round and it rains practically every day. On higher land, forests are often surrounded by clouds, hence their name of cloud forests. There are also monsoon or moist forests. These are further away from the equator where the rain does not fall in an even pattern throughout the year.

WET, WET, WET

The name is a giveaway really, but if you don't like getting wet, the rainforest is not the place for you. The weather in the lowland rainforests is very humid. There's always moisture in the air — either falling from the sky or rising as evaporation. These are ideal conditions for many plants to grow in — and they grow quickly. Each plant fights for its slice of sunlight rising higher and higher towards the sky. As a result the forest floor is a pretty dark place to be.

CROWDED HOUSE

Rainforests cover only about 6 per cent of the earth's surface, but it's believed they are home to around 50 per cent of the world's plants and animals. In just one hectare of land it's possible to spot hundreds of different species of tree, and thousands of birds, animals and insects.

◀ FROM THE GROUND UP

The rainforest is generally split into four levels, each with its own species of plants and animals. Starting at the bottom is, fairly obviously, the forest floor – the largest of the forest animals are found here. Next is the understory, which is the term for the smaller plants and young trees. Continue upwards and you come to the canopy, which means amongst the branches to you and me. Finally you get to the emergents – they're the show-offs of the tree world which grow taller than everyone else. They get more sunlight than the other trees, but are usually the first to fall down in high winds, too. Serves them right!

As jungles are such difficult places to explore we know that many of the plants and animals there are yet to be discovered. New species are being discovered all the time – who knows how many new varieties are out there.

Although the Central American rainforest is one of the smaller tropical forests, the South American Amazon rainforest is the world's largest. Together they have the biggest range of animals found anywhere on earth.

Sloths spend so much of their time resting that even plants have time to grow on them – they are covered in green algae!

▼ EAGLE-EYED PREDATOR

You may think that being able to climb to the tops of the trees would keep you safe from predators, but that's not the case here. The fearsome harpy eagle – one of the world's largest eagles – swoops over the tree tops of central and South America. It's powerful enough to hunt animals as large as monkeys.

h American Jungle

◀ THE BEAR FACTS

The popular children's book character of Paddington Bear was based on South America's spectacled bear. As you might imagine, these shy creatures don't share Paddington's fondness for marmalade sandwiches. In reality, South America's only type of bear eats fruit, nuts, plants and some small animals.

A RIVER RUNS THROUGH IT

The Amazon rainforest gets its name from the mighty Amazon River which flows for nearly 6,300 kilometres from the Andes Mountains down through the jungle to the Atlantic ocean. It may not be the world's longest (it gets beaten by the Nile) but it carries more water than any other river. It's also home to thousands of species of animals including river dolphins, turtles, anacondas and the ferocious piranha fish.

▶ TOXIC

Of course, you don't have to be big to be dangerous, and with the poison dart frog the clue to their deadly nature is in the name. The frog can make poison ooze from its skin and it's deadly enough to kill a monkey-sized animal. American Indians use the poison to tip their blow pipe darts for hunting. There are over 70 species of poison dart frog, though a few of them aren't actually poisonous. The general rule is if they're colourful, they're toxic, so watch out!

The African Jungle

Most of the African rainforest is found in the area known as central Africa. It is the second largest area of rainforest after the Amazon, and spreads over a number of different countries.

▲ JUNGLE ARMY

Even large animals have reason to fear one of the smallest predators in the jungle. Driver ants move in great swarms numbering up to millions of individuals. They have a ferocious bite, and there have been reports of driver ants eating goats, cows and even elephants!

◀ GENTLE GIANT

One animal that has suffered from a poor reputation in the past is the gorilla. Often thought to be violent creatures, these close relatives of humans are actually quite gentle and intelligent. They live in groups called troops led by the dominant male known as a silverback due to – yes, you guessed it – the grey hairs on his back.

WHO'S A PRETTY BOY THEN? ▶

Although not as vibrantly pretty as some of the macaws found in rainforests around the world, the grey parrot is one of the most talkative parrots in the world. Unfortunately, its ability to mimic sounds has also led to it becoming one of the forest's many endangered animals. Trade in these intelligent birds has been illegal for many years, but poaching still goes on.

Believe it or not, gorillas actually sleep in nests, either on the ground or in trees. They're quite loose constructions – but they do build a new one every night.

▼ TASTY

Like all rainforests, the African jungle is home to thousands of fruits and edible plants. Coffee, yams, bananas, plantains and palm oil are just a few of the foodstuffs that are valuable to people living in Africa.

LITTLE AND LARGE

You'd think that spotting an animal as big as an elephant wouldn't be so tricky – never mind a whole herd of them – but the African rainforest is so dense that it has made studying forest elephants very problematic. It's only fairly recently that scientists realised they were actually a completely different species to their larger elephant cousins which live on the African savannah.

The Asian Jungle

The rainforests of Asia cover a wide area stretching from India to Indonesia and down through New Guinea. This wide-ranging area is home to a huge variety of plants and animals.

▼ OLD MAN

If you're in Indonesia and you're really lucky you might spot an old man – but we're not talking about pensioners here. The orang-utan is often referred to as the old man of the forest. This retiring and intelligent ape is one of mankind's closest relatives, but it rarely comes down to the ground so it's difficult to see. Instead, it's happiest swinging through the trees with its long, powerful arms.

STINKER ▶

The jungles of Borneo are home to the world's largest flower. It's called the rafflesia and its flower can grow up to one metre across. But before you head off to the garden centre to try and buy one there is a major problem with this particular plant. Its size is matched by its smell – basically, it stinks of rotting meat. Not the sort of thing you want in your garden really!

▲ SPOT THE PREDATOR

Many jungle animals use camouflage to hide in the shadows – this is as true of insects as it is of big predators such as leopards and tigers. The cloud leopard's bold markings may stand out in a safari park, but in its natural home those spots match the dappled light and shade of the jungle perfectly.

▼ PASSENGERS

Plants like rafflesia are parasites – they feed off other plants. But in the Asian jungles there is another type of plant which grows on trees but isn't parasitic. They're called epiphytes and, like this bird's nest fern, they just use the trees to hitch a lift up to where the light is better.

The Asian rainforests are home to the reticulated python – the longest species of snake in the world. They can grow to be over 10 metres long!

Australian Jungle

Although the Australian rainforest is small compared with others found across the world, it doesn't mean that it's not spectacular. Australia's remoteness from other large landmasses has allowed its wildlife to evolve in unique and surprising ways.

▲ NIGHT CRAWLER

One creature found only in the Australian rainforest is the green ringtail possum which, like the tree kangaroo, spends the vast majority of its time above ground. Like many rainforest animals, it is nocturnal, which means it is active at night. The advantage of a nocturnal lifestyle is that there are fewer predators about when it is dark. During the day, the possum sleeps on a branch curled up in a tight ball.

◄ HOPPING ALONG

The last place you'd expect to see a kangaroo is in a tree, but that's exactly where you can spot them in this rainforest. There are 11 species of tree kangaroo in the world and some are so well adapted to their life in the branches they can barely hop on the ground any more.

◀ FEELING BLUE

Rainforests are home to numerous insects, and some of the most colourful are the butterflies. One of the stars of the Australian jungle is the Ulysses butterfly, or the mountain blue as it is known. Being such a vivid blue colour – and measuring about 14 centimetres across – it's one of the easier animals to spot in the rainforest.

Tree kangaroos and possums are both marsupials, which means they carry their young babies in pouches on their fronts. There is a bigger range of marsupials in Australia than anywhere else.

BEWARE OF THE PLANT

Of course, it's not just animals that can be a danger in the rainforest – sometimes the plants can cause pain and injury, too! The aptly named stinging tree produces leaves and stems which are covered in short hairs which, if touched, can stick into a person's body. What's more, the hairs are poisonous too, so on top of the cut you get an irritation which can last for months!

Jungle People

The rainforests are not just home to a dazzling array of plants and animals. Around 50 million people around the world call the jungle their home. Grouped into roughly 1,000 different tribes, these peoples have learnt how to live and adapt to such a difficult environment.

▲ ON THE MOVE

Can you imagine having no permanent place to call home? Many rainforest people, like this member of the Huli tribe from Papua New Guinea, are hunter-gatherers. They get their food by hunting for animals or collecting edible plants. These tribes move around a lot as they have to live where food can be found.

► EXTREME FARMING

When tribes like the Yanomamo of Brazil do a bit of weeding, they don't use secateurs or hoes. Instead, they employ the slash-and-burn method – chopping down trees and burning the understory. The cleared ground is then planted with fruits and edible plants. After a year or two these fields are abandoned to be reseeded by the jungle.

The name for people who belong to a certain area is indigenous people.

▲ FOUND IN THE FOREST

If you know what to look for, the rainforest is like the greatest shop in the world! It provides food, building materials, clothes and tools – and it's all free! This house, being built by a Mbuti woman from Zaire, is made from branches and leaves – a simple structure ideally suited to the Mbuti tribe's nomadic lifestyle.

DEADLY MEETING

For many tribes, their first meeting with people from Europe was a deadly one. The European explorers brought with them diseases such as measles and small pox – illnesses which the rainforest people had never encountered before and had no natural resistance to. Tragically, whole tribes were wiped out through contact with Europeans.

▼ PROTESTING

The rights of the forest peoples have often been ignored. Industry and logging have taken over large areas of the forests they called home. Now some Amazon rainforest tribes are fighting back. Their high-profile protests, which have gained the support of pop-stars like Sting, have secured the future of part of the forests for these tribes.

Hotting Up

T he world's jungles are shrinking at a phenomenal rate, and it's all down to the actions of humans. There is a real chance that the rainforests will be being totally wiped out within 50 years — and then we'll be in deep trouble! Here's why...

▼ USEFUL PLANTS

Believe it or not, many of the drugs we use today originated from plants found in the rainforest. Although indigenous people have used healing plants for years, scientists are only really discovering them now. But with the rainforests fast disappearing, so are our chances of finding more useful medicines.

▲ CARBON COPY

Plants contain a lot of carbon and when trees are felled they release this carbon into the atmosphere as carbon dioxide — a major contributor to the greenhouse effect which is causing our planet to warm up. The rainforests also absorb a significant amount of carbon dioxide, so the more trees that come down, the hotter things will be.

WASHED AWAY

Surprisingly, although rainforest trees grow very tall, the soil in the rainforest is only a few centimetres deep. This means that when the trees are gone that it is very easy for all the soil to get washed away when it rains. This in turn leads to more forest clearance to make more fields — which will then get washed away. And so it goes on.

▼ FOOD FOR THOUGHT

Fancy a monkey burger? Or a slice of roast gorilla, perhaps? Although this might sound strange, in some places in Africa, bush meat – the name given to dead jungle animals – has become a staple part of people's diets. Often this is illegal and is pushing some species of animal close to extinction.

Some environmentalists estimate that an area of rainforest the size of a football field is cleared every second!

▼ TIMBER!

The most obvious threat to the rainforests comes from logging. Huge areas of rainforest – some larger than some countries – have been cut down to create farmland and to supply the timber industry. The cleared land is used to plant soya beans or coffee, or is used as grazing land. The irony is that the rainforest soil is not actually very fertile, so all the nourishment is used up very quickly and then more land has to be cleared.

This edition published in 2011 by Arcturus Publishing Limited
26/27 Bickels Yard, 151–153 Bermondsey Street,
London SE1 3HA

Author: Paul Harrison
Designer: Talking Design, Maki Ryan, Beatriz Waller
Cover design: Maki Ryan, Beatriz Waller
Editor: Rebecca Gerlings
Illustrator (glasses): Ian Thompson

Picture credits:
NHPA: front cover; page 2, bottom; page 7; page 9, bottom; page 10,
top and bottom.
Nature Picture Library: page 3; page 5, bottom;
page 6, top; page 8; page 9, middle; page 14, top;
page 15, top and bottom.
FLPA: title page; page 4; page 5, top; page 6; page 9, top and back
cover; page 13, bottom; page 16.
Still Pictures: page 7, bottom; page 11; page 12, bottom; page 13, top
and bottom; page 14, bottom.
Jungle Photos: page 2, top.

3-D images by Pinsharp 3D Graphics

Printed in Malaysia

ISBN: 978-1-84193-391-7

CH000520US
Supplier 01, Date 0311, Print Run 759